Animals from Head to

T0014466

FISH
FROM HEAD TO TAIL

By Bill Spunter

Gareth Stevens
PUBLISHING

Please visit our website, www.garethstevens.com. For a free color catalog of all our high-quality books, call toll free 1-800-542-2595 or fax 1-877-542-2596.

Cataloging-in-Publication Data

Names: Spunter, Bill.
Title: Fish from head to tail / Bill Spunter.
Description: New York : Gareth Stevens Publishing, 2017. | Series: Animals from head to tail | Includes index.
Identifiers: ISBN 9781482449587 (pbk.) | ISBN 9781482445381 (library bound) | ISBN 9781482445268 (6 pack)
Subjects: LCSH: Fishes–Juvenile literature.
Classification: LCC QL617.2 S68 2017 | DDC 597–dc23

First Edition

Published in 2017 by
Gareth Stevens Publishing
111 East 14th Street, Suite 349
New York, NY 10003

Copyright © 2017 Gareth Stevens Publishing

Editor: Ryan Nagelhout
Designer: Katelyn E. Reynolds

Photo credits: Cover, p. 1 Madhourses/Shutterstock.com; p. 5 Artem Firsov/Shutterstock.com; p. 7 stephan kerkhofs/Shutterstock.com; p. 9 nodff/Shutterstock.com; p. 11 MattiaATH/Shutterstock.com; pp. 13, 24 (gills) Bill Perry/Shutterstock.com; p. 15 Vilainecrevette/Shutterstock.com; pp. 17, 24 (goldfish) dien/Shutterstock.com; pp. 19, 24 (bass) Beth Swanson/Shutterstock.com; p. 21 Grigorev Mikhail/Shutterstock.com; p. 23 Joe Quinn/ Shutterstock.com.

Printed in the United States of America

CPSIA compliance information: Batch #CS16GS: For further information contact Gareth Stevens, New York, New York at 1-800-542-2595.

Contents

Fish live in water.

They move by swimming.

7

Some fish have
big mouths!

They have very
round eyes.

Fish have
parts called gills.
This helps them breathe.

gills

They are many different colors.

Goldfish are very bright.

Some bass are brown.
Others are green.

Fish have fins.
They help fish swim.

Their tails are big fins!

Words to Know

bass   gills   goldfish

Index